CONTENTS

WHO'S WHO

 Bob Marley (1945–1981) Raised in the ghettos of Kingston, Jamaica, Marley became a stadium-filling reggae superstar. He is revered as a legendary songwriter and rhythm guitarist.

 Neville B. Livingston (1947–) A childhood friend of Bob Marley's, he was the percussionist and spiritual heart of the reggae group the Wailing Wailers.

 Peter McIntosh (1944–1987) The third member of the Wailers, "Tosh," as he was also known, was the most rebellious member of the group. He played lead guitar and keyboard.

 Lee Perry (1936–) Perry was an original, maverick Jamaican record producer. Originally a disk jockey, Perry helped develop reggae music with Bob Marley in the early 1970s.

 Chris Blackwell (1937–) Blackwell was a Jamaican-born, white, upper class, record producer/distributor. Through his label, Island Records, Marley gained a worldwide audience.

 Mortimo Planno (1920–2006) Mortimo was a devout Rastafarian, friend, and unofficial manager of the young Bob Marley in the late 1960s.

TROUBLE IN PARADISE

In order to understand Bob Marley, it's important to know the history of his home country: Jamaica. Native people from Guyana, in South America, had lived undisturbed on this tropical island since AD 650. Nearly 850 years later, the first Westerners came, led by Christopher Columbus. Exploring it for the Spanish, he named it Jamaica.

SLAVERY
Slaves were owned by their masters and were often mistreated. Life under slavery was hard.

JAMAICAN HISTORY

In 1655, the British captured Jamaica from the Spanish. They brought over slaves from West Africa to farm sugar plantations.

At the end of the 1700s, the value of sugarcane dropped. Sugar trading slowed and fewer slaves were needed. In 1838, they were freed.

Worker unrest in 1938 led to the creation of labor unions. This, in turn, laid the foundation for two political parties. The People's National Party (PNP) and the Jamaican Labor Party (JLP) secured Jamaican independence from Britain in 1962.

POSTWAR BOOM

Before World War II, Jamaica had an economy based on farming. After the war, the mining of bauxite and new tourism brought much-needed money to the island. However, this change in fortune caused problems.

PLAYGROUND OF THE JET SET
In the 1950s, Jamaica became a popular place for American and British tourists to visit.

LEFT BEHIND
Despite the economic boom, many thousands of Jamaicans continued to live in poverty.

COUNTRY EXODUS

From all over the country, working people flooded into the Jamaican capital, Kingston. A lucky few found jobs and relative prosperity. The rest were poor and lived in bad neighborhoods. Bob Marley was one of those people.

THE POOR

Poor people were crowded into the run-down areas west of Kingston. One of these areas was called Trench Town. Government yards were the best living spaces. These were blocks of small apartments that shared washing and toilet facilities. Homemade cardboard shacks were the lowliest. Sometimes they were built on the Dungle, a settlement that doubled as the city dump.

Daily life was brutal. Crime levels were high and there was little policing. Tourists were advised to stay away from West Kingston where the "rude boys" ruled the streets. Rude boys were knife-carrying street toughs who often fought with each other and were always ready to start a riot.

THE TRENCH TOWN EXPERIENCE
Many black Jamaicans lived painfully hard lives in conditions of grinding poverty.

RHYTHM AND ROOTS

It didn't matter if they were poor, on the weekend the residents of Kingston would gather for open-air dances in the city's public spaces. The top dance clubs would play the latest rhythm and blues music just released from America.

MUSIC PIONEERS

Competition between the promoters was fierce. In the mid 1950s, two men stood above the rest–Duke Reid and Clement "Sir Coxsone" Dodd.

When rock and roll replaced the rhythm and blues style of music as the sound of the dominant American dance scene, Reid and Dodd began looking for a way to make their own dance records. They opened recording studios. Reid opened Treasure Isle, and Coxsone opened Studio One, and they began using local musicians. Sales of their records boomed in Jamaica.

A NEW BEAT CALLED SKA

Jamaicans today still argue about who invented the style called ska at the beginning of the 1960s. But everyone agrees that it was the first truly Jamaican dance music.

Ska was a mixture of mento (Jamaican folk music), rhythm and blues, and jazz, with an emphasis on unusual beats. The fast beat drove the dancers crazy, and Jamaica soon became known as the music capital of the Caribbean.

JAMAICAN DANCEHALL KING
Only the newest, hottest, American rhythm and blues records could guarantee a packed dance floor for DJs like "Sir Coxsone" Dodd.

ROOTS OF THE RASTAFARIAN RELIGION

In 1916, a Jamaican-born black activist called Marcus Garvey made a prophecy that a black king would be crowned. In 1930, Prince Regent Ras Tafari was made emperor of Ethiopia. He was declared by Garvey's followers to be the new messiah and took the name Haile Selassie. Rastafarians, followers of Ras Tafari, believed in spiritual purity and rejected materialism. They were treated like outcasts by ordinary Jamaicans.

YOUNG BOB MARLEY

Bob Marley was born in Nine Miles, St. Ann, in Jamaica on February 6, 1945, to a black Jamaican, Cedella Marley, and her husband, a white Englishman, Norval Marley. Norval Marley, a district official, soon abandoned them and Cedella raised Bob with the help of relatives. When Bob was twelve, they went to live in Trench Town.

Cedella and Bob lived with a man named Toddy Livingston and his son, Neville. Neville and Bob became friends through a shared love of music.

When he was fifteen, Bob left school and began to work for a local welder. Encouraged by one of the other boys, he recorded some songs for producer Leslie Kong, but none was a hit.

GHETTO TRIO

Marley's first success was with a group called the Wailing Wailers. The original Wailers (Bob Marley center) were a vocal harmony group. Their first hit, "Simmer Down" (1963), was a direct appeal for their fellow Jamaicans to stay calm during a time of civil unrest.

BOB MARLEY
THE LIFE OF A MUSICAL LEGEND

OCTOBER 25, 1979. THE APOLLO THEATER, HARLEM, NEW YORK CITY.

BOB MARLEY IS THE BIGGEST STAR OF REGGAE THIS PLANET HAS EVER SEEN. HE'S HERE TO PROMOTE A MESSAGE OF PEACE AND TOGETHERNESS.

WOW, WHAT A CROWD! WHO'S PLAYING?

BOB MARLEY, OF COURSE!

BOB WHO?

BOB MARLEY! YOU KNOW THE REGGAE SUPERSTAR.

INSIDE THE THEATER...

THIS SONG GOES OUT TO THE OPPRESSED PEOPLE OF THE WORLD EVERYWHERE!

ROAR!

MARLEY'S SONG, "SIMMER DOWN," CALLED FOR THE RUDE BOYS OF TRENCH TOWN TO COOL THEIR TEMPERS. COXSONE AGREED TO SIGN THEM UP. IT WAS A HIT. BUT MARLEY BEGAN TO WORRY THAT COXSONE DIDN'T APPRECIATE THEM.

1964, GREENWICH PARK ROAD, TRENCH TOWN. NEVILLE, PETER, AND MARLEY TOOK THEIR USUAL ROUTE HOME FROM STUDIO ONE.

I CAN'T BELIEVE HE MADE US PLAY OTHER PEOPLE'S MUSIC.

IT'S NOT EXACTLY WHAT OUR AUDIENCE WANTS.

COXSONE IS INTERESTED IN HOW MUCH MONEY HE CAN MAKE OUT OF US. HE DOESN'T CARE ABOUT THE MUSIC WE WANT TO PLAY!

HEY, LOOK, THAT NURSE IS WAVING AT US.

I'M GOING OVER TO SAY HELLO.

THIS GIRL SAYS SHE HAS A VOCAL GROUP AND SHE WANTS TO SING WITH US!

SHE SHOULD TRY OUT AT COXSONE'S THEN WE'LL SEE.

SOON, THE NURSE, RITA ANDERSON, HER COUSIN, "DREAM" WALKER, AND FRIEND, MARLENE GIFFORD (AS THE SOULETTES) WERE SIGNED TO COXSONE'S STUDIO ONE. MARLEY LIKED RITA, BUT HE KEPT CRITICIZING HER.

HOLD IT! HOLD IT! YOU'RE OUT OF RHYTHM. LET'S **START AGAIN!**

LATER NEVILLE WENT OVER TO RITA.

BOB ASKED ME TO GIVE YOU THIS PERSONAL NOTE.

WHAT IS IT? ARE YOU TWO MAKING FUN OF ME?

WHAT'S WRONG WITH BOB? HE'S SO STRICT!

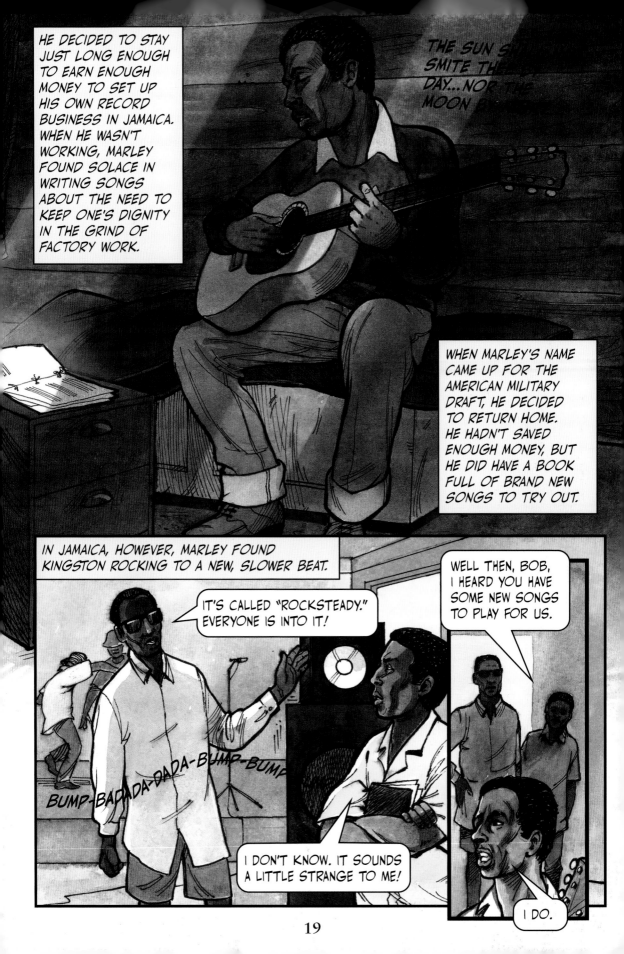

HE DECIDED TO STAY JUST LONG ENOUGH TO EARN ENOUGH MONEY TO SET UP HIS OWN RECORD BUSINESS IN JAMAICA. WHEN HE WASN'T WORKING, MARLEY FOUND SOLACE IN WRITING SONGS ABOUT THE NEED TO KEEP ONE'S DIGNITY IN THE GRIND OF FACTORY WORK.

THE SUN S... SMITE TH... DAY... NOR THE MOON B...

WHEN MARLEY'S NAME CAME UP FOR THE AMERICAN MILITARY DRAFT, HE DECIDED TO RETURN HOME. HE HADN'T SAVED ENOUGH MONEY, BUT HE DID HAVE A BOOK FULL OF BRAND NEW SONGS TO TRY OUT.

IN JAMAICA, HOWEVER, MARLEY FOUND KINGSTON ROCKING TO A NEW, SLOWER BEAT.

IT'S CALLED "ROCKSTEADY." EVERYONE IS INTO IT!

WELL THEN, BOB, I HEARD YOU HAVE SOME NEW SONGS TO PLAY FOR US.

BUMP-BADADA-DADA-BUMP-BUMP

I DON'T KNOW. IT SOUNDS A LITTLE STRANGE TO ME!

I DO.

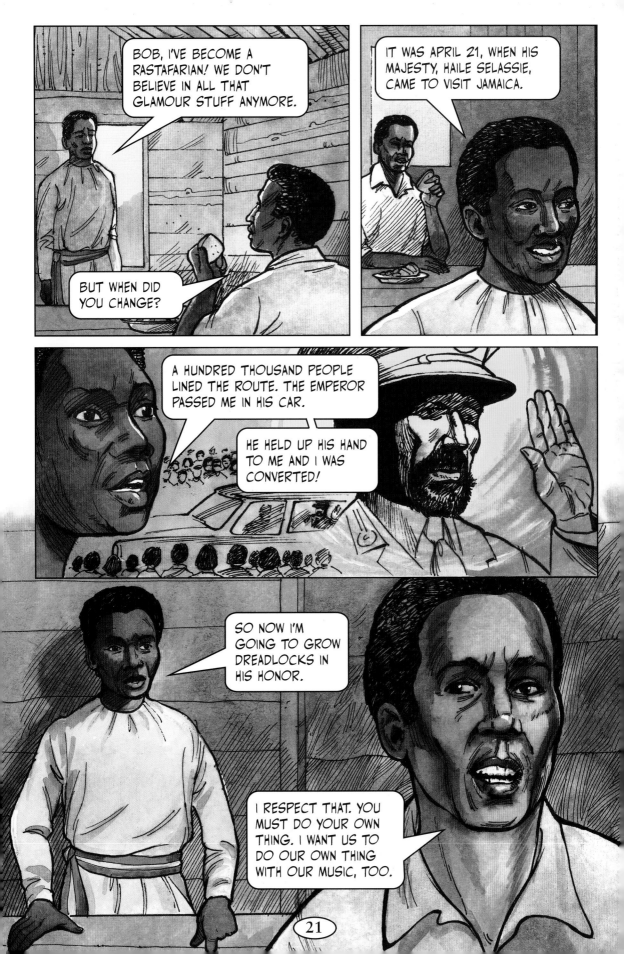

IN THE FALL OF 1966, MARLEY AND RITA FORMED THEIR OWN LABEL, WAIL 'N' SOUL, TO RECORD WAILERS' AND SOULETTES' SONGS. MARLEY BUILT A STALL OUTSIDE THE HOUSE SO THAT THEY COULD SELL RECORDS DIRECTLY TO THE PEOPLE.

COME AND GET THE LATEST HOT TUNES FROM WAIL 'N' SOUL RECORDS.

THEIR FIRST RELEASE WAS "BEND DOWN LOW" BY THE WAILERS. THE VENTURE, HOWEVER, WASN'T A SUCCESS.

BOB, WE'RE BROKE! WE'VE RUN OUT OF STOCK, AND WE OWE MONEY, AND...AND...I'M **GOING TO HAVE A BABY!**

WOW! THAT'S GREAT!

YOU KNOW, I WANT TO HAVE AS MANY CHILDREN AS THERE ARE SHELLS ON THE BEACH!

RITA HAD A GIRL THEY NAMED CEDELLA, THE FIRST OF THEIR FOUR CHILDREN. THE OTHERS WERE DAVID (ZIGGY), STEPHEN, AND STEPHANIE.

WHILE MARLEY ANTICIPATED THE JOYS OF FATHERHOOD, THE OTHER WAILERS WERE CONFRONTING COXSONE AT STUDIO ONE.

WE'RE TIRED OF BEING CHEATED BY YOU, COXSONE.

YOU'VE SUCCEEDED OFF OF OUR BLOOD AND SWEAT, MAN!

STAY BACK!

COXSONE BACKED DOWN BUT REFUSED TO PAY THEM ANY MORE MONEY.

WITH FATE SEEMINGLY AGAINST THEM, PETER AND NEVILLE HAD SOUGHT SOLACE IN RASTAFARIANISM. KEEN TO KNOW MORE, MARLEY ATTENDED A SECRET RASTA CEREMONY.

WITH NEVILLE AND PETER IN AGREEMENT, MARLEY DECIDED TO MAKE THE WAILERS INDEPENDENT OF COXSONE.

BUT WE'RE GOING TO NEED MUSICIANS!

DON'T WORRY. IT'S TAKEN CARE OF.

WAILERS, MEET THE UPSETTERS!

THE UPSETTERS WERE THE MUSICIANS OF MAVERICK JAMAICAN PRODUCER LEE "SCRATCH" PERRY. HOWEVER, PERRY HAD NEGLECTED TO PAY THE UPSETTERS FOR A RECENT TOUR.

WHEN HE FOUND OUT THAT BOB MARLEY HAD MADE THEM A BETTER OFFER...

I WILL GET BOB MARLEY!

WHEN MARLEY HEARD OF THE THREAT...

MAYBE HE SHOULD HAVE PAID THEM!

25

A MEETING WAS ARRANGED TO SETTLE THE SCORE.

BLOODSHED WAS PREDICTED.

HOWEVER, A FEW HOURS LATER...

BOYS, WE HAVE A NEW SONG, "SMALL AXE!"

WE ALSO HAVE A NEW PRODUCER. TOGETHER WE WILL BEAT THE BIG THREE!*

*THE THREE MAJOR JAMAICAN PRODUCERS WERE COXSONE, DUKE REID, AND PRINCE BUSTER.

PERRY ENCOURAGED THE WAILERS TO BE BOLD AND EXPERIMENTAL.

YOU MUST REMEMBER THAT MUSIC HAS NO RULES AND NO LIMITS!

NO LIMITS! NOW, LET'S GO!

BEGINNING IN 1969, THEY FUSED MARLEY'S RASTA-INSPIRED LYRICS, NEVILLE'S MYSTICAL PERCUSSION, AND PETER'S AGGRESSIVE GUITAR WITH THE UPSETTERS' THROBBING BEAT, IN A POWERFUL NEW STYLE CALLED *REGGAE*.

THE WAILERS' REGGAE SONGS, SUCH AS "SOUL REBEL" AND "SMALL AXE," BECAME BIG HITS. MEANWHILE, IN 1968, MARLEY HAD AUDITIONED FOR AMERICAN MANAGER DANNY SIMS AND SINGER JOHNNY NASH.

WE LIKE YOUR SONGS, BOB. WE WANT TO HELP YOU MAKE IT REALLY BIG.

THE NEXT STOP IS SWEDEN.

COOL!

SIMS ARRANGED FOR MARLEY TO STAY IN STOCKHOLM, SWEDEN, TO WRITE MATERIAL FOR A FILM SOUNDTRACK. THE TRIP FUELED MARLEY'S DESIRE TO GET HIS MUSICAL MESSAGE HEARD OUTSIDE OF JAMAICA.

IN 1972, WITH MARLEY AND THE WAILERS FIRMLY ESTABLISHED AT THE TOP OF THE JAMAICAN REGGAE SCENE, SIMS ARRANGED FOR THEM TO GO TO THE UK FOR A PROPOSED TOUR. HOWEVER, THINGS DIDN'T GO AS PLANNED.

THE TOUR IS CANCELED? OH NO, THAT MEANS WE'RE STRANDED!

COOL IT, BOYS! HAVE FAITH!

BY NOW, BOB WAS THE BAND'S ESTABLISHED LEADER. HE WAS NEGOTIATING A DEAL WITH A NEW LABEL, ISLAND RECORDS.

I HAVE HERE, SIR, THE FRUITS OF OUR LABORS.

WE NEED TO MAKE THE REGGAE SOUND APPEAL TO A ROCK AUDIENCE. I HOPE YOU DON'T MIND.

NO, THAT'S COOL, CHRIS.

AS LONG AS I CAN RELEASE MY OWN VERSION FOR THE PEOPLE OF JAMAICA.

IN 1973, "CATCH A FIRE" WAS RELEASED ON ISLAND RECORDS AND MARLEY'S NEW LABEL, TUFF/GONG.

THE WAILERS SPENT THE REST OF THE YEAR TOURING EUROPE AND AMERICA TO PROMOTE "CATCH A FIRE."

BUT HALFWAY THROUGH THEIR TOUR...

NEVILLE IS LEAVING? WHY?

HE'S HOMESICK.

NEVILLE NEVER TOURED AGAIN AS A WAILER.

IN AMERICA AS A WARM-UP ACT, THE WAILERS MANAGED TO COMPLETELY UPSTAGE THE MAIN EVENT, SLY AND THE FAMILY STONE.

SLY DOESN'T LIKE THAT.

SLY HAD THE BAND THROWN OFF THE TOUR.

BURNIN' The Wailers

AT THE END OF 1973, THE GROUP RETURNED TO THE STUDIO TO MAKE A FOLLOW-UP ALBUM FOR ISLAND. THIS TIME MARLEY DEMANDED MORE CREATIVE CONTROL. RAW IN SOUND AND REVOLUTIONARY IN SPIRIT, "BURNIN'" WAS A HIT ON ITS EUROPEAN RELEASE.

IN 1974, BLACKWELL AND TOSH CLASHED WHEN BLACKWELL REFUSED TO PRODUCE HIS SOLO PROJECT.

I QUIT THE WAILERS!

A THIRD ALBUM, "NATTY DREAD," WAS RELEASED AT THE END OF 1974. MARLEY WAS BECOMING A WORLDWIDE STAR. HE WAS SEEN AS AN INSPIRATIONAL FIGURE BY HIS OWN COUNTRYMEN, AS THE WHOLE ISLAND SEEMED TO TURN TO REGGAE OVERNIGHT.

THE RELEASE OF A LIVE ALBUM IN 1975 SEALED MARLEY'S REPUTATION AS AN INCREDIBLE LIVE PERFORMER. AT HOME HE WAS NOW REGARDED AS THE MOST IMPORTANT JAMAICAN WHO HAD EVER LIVED.

IN 1975, THE PRIME MINISTER OF JAMAICA WAS MICHAEL MANLEY, LEADER OF THE PEOPLE'S NATIONAL PARTY (PNP). HIS OPPONENT WAS EDWARD SEAGA. SEAGA WAS THE LEADER OF THE JAMAICAN LABOR PARTY (JLP).

Daily Gleaner

500 OF SEAGA'S MEN DETAINED UNDER "HEAVY MANNERS"

IN 1976, A GENERAL ELECTION WAS DUE TO BE HELD. THE JLP BEGAN USING STRONG-ARM TACTICS TO INFLUENCE VOTERS IN POOR TOWNS AGAINST THE PNP. MANLEY FEARED HE WOULD LOSE THE ELECTION AND LOCKED UP A GROUP OF SEAGA'S MEN. THIS RAISED THE THREAT OF VIOLENCE.

DESPERATE FOR A WAY TO DEFUSE THE TENSION, MANLEY SENT HIS MEN TO ASK HIS NEIGHBOR, BOB MARLEY, FOR HELP.

MICHAEL WANTS TO KNOW IF YOU WILL AGREE TO HEADLINE A FREE CONCERT FOR THE PEOPLE BEFORE THE ELECTION.

I DON'T KNOW. I MEAN, RASTAFARIANS DO NOT GET INVOLVED WITH POLITICS, YOU KNOW.

IT'S NOT FOR POLITICS. MICHAEL JUST WANTS TO COOL DOWN THE PEOPLE.

TO HELP PREVENT ANY VIOLENCE BEFORE ELECTION DAY.

IF IT WILL HELP STOP TROUBLE, I WILL DO IT!

THE CONCERT, CALLED SMILE JAMAICA, WAS ARRANGED FOR SUNDAY, DECEMBER 5.

A WEEK BEFORE THE SHOW, MARLEY TALKED WITH HIS MANAGER, DON TAYLOR, WHO HAD CONCERNS ABOUT THE TIMING OF THE CONCERT.

BOB, PEOPLE WILL THINK YOU ARE SUPPORTING MANLEY TO HELP HIM WIN THE ELECTION. YOU'RE MAKING YOURSELF A TARGET FOR HIS ENEMIES!

MAYBE, BUT IF THIS SHOW WILL HELP KEEP THE PEACE...

...THEN I MUST TAKE THAT RISK.

PNP MEMBERS POSITIONED THEMSELVES OUTSIDE THE GATES TO MARLEY'S HOUSE.

33

THE DAILY NEWS

BOB MARLEY SHOT!

ASSASSINATION ATTEMPT ON REGGAE SUPERSTAR BOB MARLEY
BULLET LODGED IN ARM
THREE OTHERS INJURED

THE PNP GUARDS HAD DISAPPEARED. THEN UNKNOWN GUNMEN HAD INVADED THE GROUNDS OF MARLEY'S HOUSE. RITA WAS WOUNDED.

ON SUNDAY, DECEMBER 5, AFTER BEING RELEASED FROM THE HOSPITAL, MARLEY STAYED AT A SECRET HIDEOUT IN THE BLUE MOUNTAINS. DURING HIS STAY, HE REASONED WITH HIS ADVISERS ABOUT WHAT TO DO NEXT.

THE PEOPLE BEHIND THE ATTACK WANTED TO SILENCE YOUR VOICE. IF YOU DON'T DO THE CONCERT, THEY'VE WON!

NO, BOB, YOU SHOULDN'T GO. IT'S TOO DANGEROUS. YOU COULD STILL GET HURT!

THE SOUNDS OF THE CONCERT WERE BEING RELAYED BY WALKIE TALKIE.

HERE, AT THE NATIONAL HEROES CIRCLE, A CROWD OF FIFTY THOUSAND ORDINARY JAMAICANS HAVE GATHERED TO PAY TRIBUTE TO THEIR OWN HERO, BOB MARLEY.

OKAY, WE NEED TO GET THE BAND TOGETHER.

THERE ARE NO POLITICS HERE! FOR THE LOVE OF THE PEOPLE I WILL SING ONE SONG.

BY THE TIME MARLEY REACHED THE STAGE, OVER EIGHTY THOUSAND PEOPLE WERE IN THE CROWD.

THE SONG WAS A HEARTFELT PLEA FOR JAMAICAN UNITY, WITH WORDS BASED ON A SPEECH BY EMPEROR HAILE SELASSIE.

...AND WE WILL TRIUMPH WITH GOOD OVER EVIL!

AFTER THE SONG, MARLEY KEPT GOING AND PERFORMED FOR NINETY MINUTES. AT THE END, HE SHOWED HIS INJURY TO THE CROWD...

SEE MY WOUND?

...AND MOCKED THE GUNMEN WHO HAD ATTACKED HIM.

HA! HA! HA!

MICHAEL MANLEY WON THE ELECTION ON DECEMBER 16.

1977, PARIS, FRANCE.

OUCH! NOT AGAIN!

MARLEY HAD DAMAGED HIS RIGHT TOE YEARS EARLIER. NOW, IT HAD HAPPENED AGAIN, RIGHT IN THE MIDDLE OF A EUROPEAN TOUR TO PROMOTE HIS NEW ALBUM, CALLED "EXODUS."

YOU SHOULD SHOW THAT TO A DOCTOR.

IT'S DEVELOPED INTO WHAT LOOKS LIKE A CANCER.

MR. MARLEY, THE SAFEST THING WOULD BE TO AMPUTATE.

NO WAY! NO RASTAFARIAN WILL BE AMPUTATED.

AMPUTATION WAS AGAINST THE RASTAFARIAN CREED. MARLEY REFUSED TREATMENT AT THE LONDON CLINIC AND FLEW TO MIAMI TO GET A SECOND OPINION.

HIS FOOT WAS TREATED BUT NOT REMOVED. MARLEY HEARD OF SOME DISTURBING DEVELOPMENTS AT HOME.

THE PNP IS REPORTED TO BE EXECUTING DEFENSELESS JLP PARTY WORKERS. THIS HAS SPARKED RUMORS OF A POSSIBLE ATTEMPT BY EDWARD SEAGA TO TAKE CONTROL OF THE GOVERNMENT BY ARMED FORCE.

MIAMI, 1978. BUCKY MARSHALL OF THE PNP AND CLAUDIE MASSOP OF THE JLP CAME TO SEE MARLEY WITH A PLEA.

IT MUST BE SOMETHING SERIOUS TO BRING YOU TWO TOGETHER!

JAMAICA NEEDS YOUR HELP, BOB!

WE HAVE TO PREVENT CIVIL WAR!

WE'RE PUTTING ON A PEACE CONCERT, CALLED ONE LOVE, TO PROMOTE A TRUCE.

FOR IT TO BE MEANINGFUL, WE NEED YOU TO BE THE MAIN ATTRACTION.

OKAY, BUT NO POLITICS. REMEMBER WHAT HAPPENED LAST TIME!

ON FEBRUARY 26, BOB MARLEY LANDED AT NORMAN MANLEY AIRPORT IN KINGSTON, JAMAICA.

ONE LOVE! ONE HEART! LET'S GET TOGETHER AND FEEL ALRIGHT.

MARLEY'S UNOFFICIAL NATIONAL ANTHEM FROM 1963 ECHOED ACROSS THE CITY.

THAT NIGHT, AFTER A CHANT SESSION AT THE NATIONAL HEROES STADIUM, MARLEY SPOKE WITH HIS BRETHREN.

TENSIONS BETWEEN THE PARTIES ARE WORSE THAN EVER BEFORE.

SOMEONE HAS TO DO SOMETHING, OR THE COUNTRY WILL TEAR ITSELF APART!

TWO MONTHS LATER, ON APRIL 22, 1978, AT THE ONE LOVE PEACE CONCERT, MARLEY PERSUADED THE PRIME MINISTER, MICHAEL MANLEY, AND OPPOSITION LEADER, EDWARD SEAGA, TO SHAKE HANDS IN FRONT OF THE TV CAMERAS AND TWENTY THOUSAND STUNNED JAMAICANS.

THE HANDSHAKE WAS REPORTED AROUND THE WORLD AND SECURED MARLEY'S REPUTATION AS A POWERFUL AGENT FOR PEACE. HE WAS AWARDED A PEACE MEDAL BY THE UNITED NATIONS.

THE APOLLO THEATER, NEW YORK CITY, 1979. AFTER "SLAVE DRIVER," BOB LAUNCHED INTO A NEW SONG, "ZIMBABWE," WRITTEN FOR THE FREEDOM FIGHTERS IN AFRICA.

BROTHER YOU'RE RIGHT...SO RIGHT. WE'LL HAVE TO FIGHT! WE'LL HAVE TO FIGHT! WE'LL HAVE TO FIGHT! FIGHTING FOR OUR RIGHTS!

BOB MARLEY WAS THE ONLY ACT INVITED TO ATTEND THE ZIMBABWE INDEPENDENCE CEREMONIES. THE ZIMBABWEANS KNEW THE WORDS TO HIS SONGS BETTER THAN THEIR NATIONAL ANTHEM. MARLEY WAS REVERED AS A WORLDWIDE PEACE BROKER.

COME TOGETHER, ZIMBABWE!

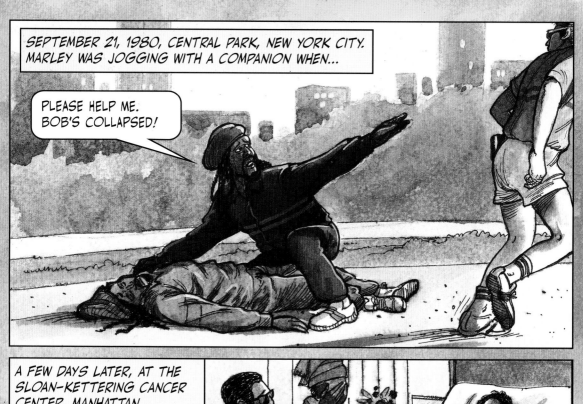

SEPTEMBER 21, 1980, CENTRAL PARK, NEW YORK CITY. MARLEY WAS JOGGING WITH A COMPANION WHEN...

PLEASE HELP ME. BOB'S COLLAPSED!

A FEW DAYS LATER, AT THE SLOAN-KETTERING CANCER CENTER, MANHATTAN...

I'M AFRAID THAT THE CANCER IN YOUR FOOT HAS SPREAD TO YOUR LIVER, LUNGS, AND BRAIN.

MARLEY WAS GIVEN TEN WEEKS TO LIVE.

IN 1981, IN MIAMI, MARLEY WAS NEAR THE END. HE ASKED TO SEE HIS SONS. RITA'S BOYS, ZIGGY AND STEPHEN, CAME TO HIS BEDSIDE.

STEPHEN, REMEMBER, MONEY CAN'T BUY LIFE.

ZIGGY, ON YOUR WAY UP, TAKE ME UP, AND ON YOUR WAY DOWN, DON'T LET ME DOWN.

ON MAY 11, 1981, BOB MARLEY DIED. HE WAS 36 YEARS OLD. HIS BODY WAS TAKEN BACK TO JAMAICA WHERE HIS FUNERAL WAS ATTENDED BY A THIRD OF THE JAMAICAN POPULATION.

BOB MARLEY WAS FINALLY LAID TO REST IN A SPECIALLY BUILT MAUSOLEUM AT HIS BIRTHPLACE, NINE MILES, IN THE QUIET COUNTRYSIDE OF ST. ANN, JAMAICA.

THE END

TIME WILL TELL

One month before he died, Bob Marley was awarded the Jamaican Order of Merit. It was the highest honor his country could bestow upon him. However, Marley isn't just remembered by the world as a Jamaican national hero.

LEGENDARY LYRICS

Bob Marley's music has been released many times since his death. It continues to inspire feelings of strength and dignity in many people the world over.

Marley's lyrics are what makes his music so appealing. Most of the lyrics tell stories of struggle in everyday life. Listeners enjoy the songs because they have shared the experiences and can relate to them.

PEACEFUL CONNECTION

Marley was committed to his African roots but desired to reach audiences of every creed and color. He made the connection through a simple message of peace. It continues to be understood by people of all races in countries around the world.

SELECTED DISCOGRAPHY

These are the albums Bob Marley and the Wailers recorded between 1972 and 1981 for Island Records.

Catch a Fire: 1973
Burnin': 1973
Natty Dread: 1974
Live! Bob Marley & the Wailers: 1975
Rastaman Vibration: 1976
Exodus: 1977
Kaya: 1978
Babylon by Bus: 1978
Survival: 1979
Uprising: 1980
Confrontation: 1983 (posthumous release)

CHEERING FOR THE UNDERDOG

Marley wanted to fight for those who were "rejected by society." Growing up in an area where groups such as the Rastafarians and the poor were outsiders, Marley understood what it was like not to be accepted. Even when he was famous, he never forgot about his family and friends back in Trench Town. Marley was a different kind of superstar, one who spoke up for people cast out by society. He remembered his humble roots.

MUSICAL LEGEND

The reggae music scene is still waiting for another performer as inspiring as Bob Marley to grace the global stage.

GLOSSARY

acetate A recording disk coated with a fiber called cellulose acetate that was used before CDs were invented.

amputate To remove a limb by cutting it off.

assassination The wounding or killing of a person, often secretly, and always planned. People are often assassinated for political reasons.

bloodshed Violence.

brotherhood A friendliness felt toward people with whom one has something in common, such as nationality or culture.

ceremony A special celebration.

compelling When something is powerfully fascinating.

emperor The ruler of an empire.

fused When two or more things, such as musical styles, are merged.

Grounation A celebration held every year on April 21 in honor of Haile Selassie, the central figure in Rastafarianism. Feasts, dancing, celebrations, and meditations mark the occasion.

maverick An independent individual who refuses to go along with the views of others.

meditation A deeply thoughtful state where an individual concentrates on his or her breathing or repeating a few words to increase his or her spiritual awareness.

mystical Something that cannot be explained through logic or reason.

negotiate To talk with another person or other people in order to find a solution to a problem.

percussion The striking of an instrument to produce a musical sound.

Rastafarian A person who follows the Rastafarian way of life. Rastafarianism was named after Ras Tafari, the name of Haile Selassie before he was crowned emperor of Ethiopia.

reggae Popular style of Jamaican music that combines rock, soul, and native styles.

rehearsal A practice session before a performance.

stranded To be left alone and helpless, often with no transport.

sugarcane A tall, thick type of grass that grows in the tropical parts of South East Asia. It is a source of sugar.

throbbing To beat with a strong rhythm.

truce A peaceful agreement following a period of disagreement or unrest. It is usually politically motivated.

union A group with a particular cause. Workers' unions exist to protect the rights of their members within the workplace.

unrest A state of unease or dissatisfaction.

upstage When a person directs attention away from someone else and toward himself or herself.

FOR MORE INFORMATION

ORGANIZATIONS

Bob Marley Museum
56 Hope Street
Kingston
Jamaica West Indies
Tel: (876) 927-9152
E-mail: marleyfoundation@cwjamaica.com
Web site: http://www.bobmarley-foundation.com/museum.html

FOR FURTHER READING

Dolan, Sean. *Bob Marley* (Black Americans of Achievement). Langhorne, PA: Chelsea House Publications, 1996.

Haskins, Jim. *One Love, One Heart: A History of Reggae.* New York, NY: Jump at the Sun, 2002.

Heinrichs, Ann. *Jamaica* (True Books). New York, NY: Children's Press, 2003.

Kallen, Stuart A. *The History of Reggae* (Music Library). Chicago, IL: Lucent Books, 2005.

Marley, Cedella, Gerald Hausman, and Mariah Fox (illustrator). *The Boy from Nine Miles: The Early Life of Bob Marley* (Young Spirit Books). Charlottesville, PA: Hampton Roads Publishing Company, 2002.

Marley, Cedella (compiler), and Gerald Hausman (compiler). *56 Thoughts from 56 Hope Road: The Sayings and Psalms of Bob Marley.* Charlottesville, PA: Hampton Roads Publishing Company, 2002.

Morris, Dennis. *Bob Marley. A Rebel Life. A Photobiography.* London, England: Plexus, 1999.

INDEX

Web Sites

Due to the changing nature of Internet links, the Rosen Publishing Group, Inc., has developed an online list of Web sites related to the subject of this book. This site is updated regularly. Please use this link to access the list:

http://www.rosenlinks.com/grbi/boma